Wilf had a rod and a net.

Let's go.

Wilf and Dad got to the river.

"We can fish in that bit," said Dad.

"Let's get fishing," said Wilf.

I see fish in this deep bit.

"Let's feed the fish," said Dad.

"I can feel a fish," said Wilf.

"Reel it in, then," said Dad.

It was not a fish.
It was a lot of weed.

"I can feel a fish," said Dad.

Dad got his feet wet.

Wilf got his feet wet.

“Get the net,” said Dad.

It was an eel.

Dad let the eel go.

“We got an eel and wet feet,” said Wilf. “But no fish.”